UNIVERSAL

By

Krishna DSRR

This book is just based on my understanding of this Universe and inspired by thoughts of Swami Vivekananda and Rama Krishna Math. I would like to create a positive world where we know what is happening in this Universe and what must be done to have a further positive and prosperous world. This book can make everyone know many happening ideas and can make them get a new Idea.__Krishna DSRR

TABLE OF CONTENTS

1. UNIVERSAL -----   7

UNIVERSAL

To The People Of This Universe,

Once an idea goes into this world the change starts though it may take time. Its only because this world must be ready to receive and apply that Idea. Here is an Example: In daily life watching movies is a favorite pass time for many of us. Some times we don't like movies with new story but after watching a few times we start liking those movies understanding new and upcoming people characteristic developments in our society. Like this way these new and upcoming ideas in all aspects of our lives need to be understood and need to be required by our world. So just till then you need to wait. When the required moment comes, you will change this whole world with your mind-blowing Idea.

Hence, give brilliant ideas to change this world positively or negatively because both can be answered with opposite which leads to updating ourselves as well. Be ready for punishment when it comes to negative because negative gets negative results. But who create remedy for a negative idea will get positive result as usual as an appreciation. Like this we make this world grow better and better. If we leave an idea out then our brain thinks to get another. These Ideas can make us get Name, Money. So, throw as many ideas as you can into this world to witness as many changes as we can before finishing this average 100 years human life like land line to Mobile, Computer to Tablet,etc list goes on in all aspects of life.__Krishna DSRR

1.   If government can give food, education for free to the poor families & children, Parents will start buying things with their savings of their earnings like TV, Fridge,

Computers, Land, Can build/buy a house like that this buying will go unending as after education children also get jobs. Government gets income through tax on those things involved in buying. As we have lot of population in our world we get more than what we spent.

2. If we start taking money as deposits like chit fund business or to pay interest for their savings many start using bank accounts, on-line banking & digital money. We can have more benefits from these like having lot of money to invest in different industries, etc....

All these can be welfare schemes from governments for poor people.__Krishna DSRR

We are just humans because we can't show, do magics to attract people and help people. Therefore, we have to think about all possible ways to win large number of people helping them excel in their lives though we hurt a few. But a few leaders from all walks of life have not been helping many considering to be partial towards a few people Interests &

Egos. It ruins them, their nation and more importantly whole world. As many business people have got to wait for opposite leaders to be in power to get approvals for their businesses to start with new projects. By helping others giving permissions for new projects without showing Caste, Creed and Party centric partiality, we can prove again that all religions said and want from us is "Be Good and Do Good."   If our leaders don't give permissions to some businesses we lose taxes from those business people and jobs for common people for those 5 years Or more. There can be a cycle of developments be stopped because of that particular leader's partiality. We also can help others in giving Spiritual, Financial, Social, Family running knowledge which lead us have a wonderful world. __Krishna DSRR

Some of the rich feel if we let poor become rich they loose their identity and respect but they don't know if poor people become rich, rich people can become more rich than before because when poor have the opportunity to become rich then rich have more opportunities to become more rich as they got every resource to do any new business, to cash any new development to become bigger than they were to have more respect than before. Some of the politicians also feel the same way if they allow poor become rich there won't be any problems to solve to get votes from but they can't observe one thing that In the most rich America also there are problems to solve to get votes from people for their politicians. This thinking is there with some upper middle class people also. Lets all hope to have world full of rich people who can have all basic needs answered well, and can have good, prosperous life. Now we have poor people in this world though we have rich, upper middle class, middle class, lower middle class, poor, very poor,etc classes in those poor people where they fight for everything. We hope to see all these classes will be like Super rich class, rich upper middle class, rich middle class, rich lower middle class, rich poor class, rich very poor class. These classes in rich people in this world where everything provided richly enough positively towards poverty free equipping finance when needed, Physically fit having required exercise, Mentally fit knowing about the strength with in you. It only happens when we are rich enough to have all required basic needs fulfilled only. I hope to see a Financially, Physically, Mentally Positive society throughout this world. __Krishna DSRR

Migrating to rich countries like America can make many become rich Financially, Socially with acquired knowledge and allow many have lot of democratic freedom which allow them become world citizens who can have exposure to whole world and it's cultures, become Liberal getting good skills like Logical thinking, Questioning, Confidence to achieve any thing being in an opportunities filled, encouraging nation. All these they can't get in developing countries. They can even support Families, Relatives, Friends,etc financially, morally. Of course in developing countries we got lot of opportunities to start new businesses if we have enough investment according to new developments especially in highly populated countries like India to cater their needs.

Both countries become more friendly to each other which benefit both in return. Only Skilled, Intelligent people must be allowed to rich intelligent country like America to avail all opportunities. And those can make many become skilled, intelligent to fill this world with intelligent, skilled, hard working, logical thinkers and cultured people as many migrated people became very successful in their respective professions who have been making this world have more like them as well. So Rich countries can be proud (can announce) for producing great people. But must be careful about some problems of mixed culture. __Krishna DSRR from '4 STORIES- 2FME'

Building IT parks, Companies, Wide cum Ring roads to connect areas&cities, Airports, Resorts, Amusement parks, and Developing famous Temples&Historic tourist spots, Water projects to answer the needs of newly developing areas... Trough Urbanization developing possible twin cities creates wealth making poor people become rich selling or holding their land for starting new businesses. Using all round development of a newest planned Eco-friendly city of Parks & Lakes, and consists of all required businesses to have lot of jobs, own businesses for poor, middle class through shopping malls, Shops, and big companies by rich... Government can build bunch of shops, Shopping malls for poor people to do different businesses, and many benefits happen for government, Business men and people. Our leaders can become gods by serving   all   classes   of   people   in   this way.__Krishna DSRR

Business Men/Women can adopt many Villages, Slums to make those be developed in all aspects. As they help those villages, slums in all-round development, those people start buying their products. So they can open new small branches, shops of their products to earn money, regular customers for their products, etc from more people than those villages, slums because they are doing good for poor people. When it comes to IT & other industries they can adopt villages, slums offering basic amenities, in return their or their parents name to that village, slum or streets of those. So that village, slum or street will be named after the person who adopted them. So all business men can Serve&Earn people to live even after death.__Krishna DSRR.

Churches, Mosques, Temples and rich God men/Women, preachers can adopt many villages, slums to make those Spiritually, Financially, Socially, Family strong by making them be developed in all aspects. As they are helping those villages, slums in all-round development, those start following that religion- Church, Temple, Mosque & Baba, Preacher, So they can open new Church, Temple, Mosque & Ashram, etc to earn money as donations, spiritual, financial followers,etc. from more people than those villages, slums and even from rich people because they have been doing good for poor people and rich people also need spirituality. Hence, all religions, God men/Women can Serve&Earn people.__Krishna DSRR from '4 STORIES- 2FME'

LAND<we live on, we get food grain, we get annual income selling it after 1 or 2 years from buying time importantly in developing cities (can be Flats, Apartments)without much hard work, we build houses to get rent, we give it to our children proudly to make them happy. So land is every thing for many and possessing land gives confidence, lot of happiness as well.__Krishna DSRR.

In many families only one person works, rest all are dependent on him. In some families one person becomes successful and the rest of the family tree, later generations live on the results of his hard work. Its really high time they also have got to start a new industry to generate jobs. Royal rich, Business Rich families can give loans to new innovative ideas for startups. They can use their whole family tree in creating startups owning major share in those. In that way many owners from family tree owning many companies. And new entrepreneurs with new innovative ideas to lead new generations. In this process of wealth creation, Its really important to remember creating discoveries, new innovative as many industries as we can which generate more jobs as well. __Krishna DSRR

Getting knowledge through News papers, Subject books, Internet, etc gives confidence to our brain to get Ideas to achieve any thing, and Having emotional journey through watching movies, Reading stories gives confidence to our heart to face any situation by having many people experiences from movies, Stories.__Krishna DSRR

17

Every one in this universe including planets like our own earth has their own problems but problems varies according to our financial, social status. Every second of our life comes with a problem to solve like waking up early is a problem for some, vice versa. We have been solving many number of problems daily from morning to night. We are perfect men/women with lot of practice to face any problem which don't take much time than a second, minute, hour, day, month, and a year not our whole life. But sticking with only one problem for more time ruins our life. Lets move forward solving all encountered problems one by one to have new one.__Krishna DSRR

Many common people are being robbed of their ideas and are being cheated with wrong excuses. It is pretty evident in film industry of stories but its been going on in every industry. It is one of the main reasons why we have not been giving great inventors, discoveries now-a-days to this world though we have lot of population -- most of them are Adaptable, Hard working, Ethical, spiritually strong & intelligent through hard work. World is on a hope to see great people from Politics,

Film industry, Business world, etc worlds who can create, encourage people of new ideas without robbing them by claiming ideas as theirs having false ego which has been harming them and world as well. Can you please create an encouraging atmosphere as discouraging atmosphere has been killing intelligence of many people. If you start it from noted movie industry, politics, IT industries then there will be a revolutionized change in this world. That change can make this world have more inventions, discoveries to fulfill people needs.__Krishna DSRR

We are Humans so we must act systematically not like any other species in this Universe. Those don't have brains hence follow desires. We got brains and a compassionate heart, therefore we can create a perfect system and even can recreate new world. __ Krishna DSRR

Every one must come to serve people but not to do politics because DEMOCRACY means serving people, So those who serve people must come to contest in elections, those who serve people must stay as leaders otherwise they must be thrown out by people from leadership.

Every wanna be leader must have done lot of social service or He must have served through protests, agitations achieving people's demands through a political party or candidates from social organizations as they have been fighting for people from years, they know every possible solution for the problems of people. He must be very familiar with his contesting area by visiting several times to solve their problems.

Every candidate must be from good characterized background who can go to people regularly to know their problems to solve but not from rich business, royal, criminal background people as they can or is a chance of earning more money than they possess by influencing people. They have been influencing people killing democratic spirit of serving people creating a kings rule where people serve leaders(Ex: VIP culture).

Every leader must be questioned, must visit their area for at least a whole week in every month to answer, to solve their people problems and To make sure all well fare schemes are reaching poor people.

He, his staff must be available 24/7 to solve people problems.

Well fare schemes, Ideas to earn money for those well fare schemes must be a eligibility criteria for choosing a candidate as a leader.

There must be recall system, if any leader commits a mistake, he must be recalled by electing new leader.

Constitution must be changed regularly as per the changing rule of 30   years   when   its written   according   to   present,   future generations.

Above all or a few can be considered to implement to get great appreciation from people.__Krishna DSRR

Giving loans to poor farmers to buy latest equipment and to follow organic farming and write off those loans if required will help lost poor Farmers due to different reasons (Natural disasters or etc). Banks and Government get benefit in terms of interest, taxes when money in circulation while buying and selling farming needs. Benefited farmers through write off when Government have lot of money can buy new household items. Government get taxes. We can see it as a Cycle which help all.__Krishna DSRR

Building roads can make us have transport to the whole world. World will have communication with that left Village or Tribe or Small town. Those people can easily go to hospitals when in need, can go to Market to buy house hold items, can go to Shopping malls to buy clothes, can go to Schools/Colleges, Can go to watch Movies, Parks/Historic places/ all sorts of entertaining, learning, earning places to visit or live having jobs.__Krishna DSRR

Be like Water different colors according to located ground color, Flow like Water facing Mountains, Higher grounds and finding another way through lower ground to reach Sea, Stay like Water, Give life like Water, Make others drown like Water with Cyclone/Tsunami when bad grows in the Society and Pollution grows in water in different forms like most importantly Plastic waste though it has been good to humans.__Krishna DSRR

In Hindu religion we got many gods and every one got their own story. Bad, Good, all types. So people can live happily justifying themselves giving examples from gods. Hence be confident and do whatever you do confidently. Result will be according to our hard work. Because of much hard work (Involves Planning, Execution) even some bad people can always escape from Police though they do mistakes. If you do good you will be revered as a holy man.__Krishna DSRR

In India we can find all types of people who follow all different types of customs, traditions. As they have many Religions, Castes, Creed. Therefore they don't need to travel whole world to know and see different color, types of people. There in India itself we can find different types of color (Black, Brown, Yellow, White), relationships (Long holy marital relationship, Live in/Crush/One night stand, etc.), different weathers (Cold in Kashmir at Himalayas, Hot/Mild in other regions, Down fall in Maghalaya State, Forest area, Deserts, Old historical forts, New Hi-tech Cities, Zoo Parks, Bird Sanctuaries, Flower parks, Fruit parks, Etc, Etc many.__Krishna DSRR

23

Love has no language hence many fall in love but to achieve or to rise in love we need to know at least lover's body language. If you know more than that to impress your Girl Friend, Soon, you will learn how to impress this whole intelligent world.__Krishna DSRR

If you fail in love, don't worry. Be positive. Go to Library you will find many love failures. Engage yourself in reading different types of books added to college subjects. You can get lot of inspiration, knowledge and a positive emotional journey to achieve any thing in this Universe. Movies also can help you get motivated, educated and can give you emotional journey to be successful.__Krishna DSRR

Don't get lost in this infinite Universe, be yourself. Don't get lost in infinite Love by lover, be yourself. Don't get lost in infinite affection by children, be yourself. Don't get lost in infinite financial issues, be yourself. Don't get lost in infinite pleasure of upbringing grandchildren, be yourself. Don't get lost in infinite pain of regret for being proved wrong of decisions in past, be yourself of conscious.__Krishna DSRR

Likes & Comments, Appreciation & Criticism are part of life. These come from Morning till Mid Night. What matters is our improvement in finding new ways and lessons we learnt while achieving whatever we want.__Krishna DSRR

We generally run after something like Money, Name, opp sex, etc but if we run after our selves means if we know our selves every thing will come most importantly Happiness will come. So, know about yourself first. World will know about you later, definitely.__Krishna DSRR

Nowadays apps are ruling our world daily creating confusion, Irritation with -Updates, New ones. Many apps for one purpose. Oh, what the hell of these apps. Wasting our time? But many are giving food(task) to our Brain which makes us use our brain much more than usual to be as intelligent as we can viewing whole world closely, comfortably and Precisely.__Krishna DSRR

To control power(Electricity) we got switches, regulators, etc. To control our brain we got our soul as a switch and regulator. So start using our switch and regulator then you can do wonders. Meditation, Yoga can help us a lot to use our switch.__Krishna DSRR

We got Holy books, many personality development books which can inspire us have a good, prosperous life but many people are negative thinkers as they don't know what is there in those books. Please let all know what is there in all those books.__Krishna DSRR

What you give that you get. So, give good to this world in response you get great from this world or else you will definitely be doomed. So, be careful to be a good human being. __Krishna DSRR

"Note it down, note it down",,,,we used to hear in our schools from our beloved teachers but now our mobiles have been asking silently providing Ms Office, Note, etc to Note it down (required things)for our own good. We must utilize the available, but ignored resources to excel in life.__Krishna DSRR

Concern, Recognition make others feel happy and responsible. If we don't have both from this world, this world gets an enemy to fight. Hence, show some concern towards, and recognize others.__Krishna DSRR

Having a few Intelligent, Good friends is far better than being a good friend to many. First case: Saves and gives great life. Second case: Wastes and ruins good life.__Krishna DSRR

Have control over your senses then you can win any thing in life. Generally we ignore our senses when we have all at perfect condition using/depending on only one. If we see a disabled person we come to know how he uses his rest of the senses. Hence, practice controlling senses to be a successful person.__Krishna DSRR

So, Therefore, Hence, Thus, Because, etc must be used, thought to do good getting positive perception of every thing, then there won't be any reason to commit a mistake.__Krishna DSRR

Water < Gives life as drinking water, gives food

as water for cultivated land, gives beautiful & life saving nature, gives comfort as house hold water to wash clothes & utensils etc, gives inspiration flowing through downs avoiding highs as to find a way towards destination. So, save as much water as you can using water harvesting methods to make this earth a beautiful & life saving cum giving. Don't let it to be in Sea than on or in our Earth.__Krishna DSRR

Name is being called by people and Fame is being remembered by people. Name is given by parents as their responsibility being parents and Fame is given by people as their responsibility for your hard work, good character which showed great results. Therefore, have Fame to make your parents feel proud and children be proud or responsible to earn much Fame while continuing present.__Krishna DSRR

Have an attitude of 'Can' before, while doing 'Good' though its very difficult and 'Can't' before doing 'Bad' though it's very easy and profitable. Then we can have a good world which is a Heaven on earth. Which means we can live in Heaven even before death. After death when you reach heaven you can say "We have better heaven on earth than you". Then they will come to earth to be in Heaven or not so heaven in contrast.__Krishna DSRR

Sharing Ideas make you have more Ideas, sharing emotions make you have more emotions, sharing experiences make you have more experiences, So the more you share the more you will get.__Krishna DSRR

"Knowing everything in detail of others will make us learn to win them and make us know our self well."__Krishna DSRR

"Flowers, Opp sex wake up the sensitivity with in us, give us lot of pleasure with a smile on our face, So have them around you".__Krishna DSRR

Birth day to Death day. What do you do between both make others celebrate your Birthday, remember your Death day forever. Therefore do something Unique.__Krishna DSRR

When you know that you are going to die soon, you become philosophical, attentive, work hard to finish all responsibilities and serve others to get good name but if you do the same thing regularly you will have lot of good reasons to smile before dying and this world have more great people.__Krishna DSRR

Great, Good, Excellent, etc adjectives are there but to have one of them, you need to struggle a lot and to keep that adjectives you need to struggle more than before.__Krishna DSRR

Blame the wrong people, appreciate good people or else nothing goes forward in this world and your life becomes nothing.__Krishna DSRR

LAND<we live on, we get food grain, we get annual income selling it after 1 or 2 years from buying time importantly in developing cities (flats,apartments)without much hard work, we build houses to get rent, we give it to our children proudly to make them happy. So land is every thing for many and possessing land gives confidence, lot of happiness as well.__Krishna DSRR from '4 STORIES- 2FME'

Getting knowledge through News papers, Subject books, Internet, etc gives confidence to our brain to get Ideas to achieve any thing and Having emotional journey through watching movies, Reading stories gives confidence to our heart to face any situation by having many people experiences from movies, stories.__Krishna DSRR

Don't quit especially while doing a good deed because it gives you many problems while doing it, but later changes many lives positively giving you everything and long lasting fame.__Krishna DSRR

Many prefer to follow a few principles, But we need to update our selves according to present situation or else we will be out of date. Updating ourselves in every aspect will make us become better person, successful person in our professions and we end up dying as a great person.__Krishna DSRR

Being a patient listener having Intelligently, emotionally good balance will make us get the situation into our hands. If we don't have patience we ruin our chances forever. So be careful of your thoughts and feelings.__Krishna DSRR

Can we edit our lives? If yes, what will you edit/remove?

My answer: I will edit all of my bad past which is effecting my present and will effect my future. Of course, it seems bit too optimistic, but yes I am a common man who hope a lot to happen but nothing happens because I can't chase fate created by bad past to win. And what about you? Will you edit your bad painful love affair, a fight with your Friend/Relative/Father/Brother/Sister, or A bad dialogue which is effecting your life or complete past by forgetting/ignoring/acting as if didn't do/correcting it. Which one do you edit?. Or Doing pretty good deeds in present can cover up our past and can give us enormous future. What do you do?__Krishna DSRR

If we do a mistake we get the inevitable bad result but we generally try to avoid that punishment and find some one to be responsible for our mistakes. Some go any extent to create bad people than him to show them as an example. In this process many are becoming bad people. This way he even ruining the whole system which result in huge loss for our nation and this whole world.__Krishna DSRR

Poor, Common, Lower Middle class, Middle class, Upper Middle class are the main voters who look for welfare schemes from Government and elect the government which provide more welfare schemes for them. These include publicity mongers Youth, Handicapped, Widows, Old aged getting pensions,etc. Rich, Super rich people generally don't go to election center to vote as they don't care about any party as they have been working in private sectors Ex: I.T, Call centers, B.P.Os, Manufacturing Industries, Small scale industries, Own businesses, Own Shops in Shopping malls, etc though their businesses can be affected by ruling party decisions because tax percentages and Bank loans are decided based on our countries economical status. Sometimes ruling party can change tax system like G.S.T and Loan methods. Moreover these people always busy with their jobs, businesses and some traveling around the world, living some where else leaving Native place where they got Voting right. Opinions vary from one to another but Old aged, Handicapped, Widows, Youth, talk a lot about parties and their ruling hence specially mentioned from Poor people, Common people, Lower Middle class, Middle Class, Upper Middle class(Including Government employees) are the reliable voters to get votes. But parties must think about all to get 100% voting. And must make rich invest in different new businesses encouraging ideas from Talented, Good people to have Inventions, Discoveries which can change the face of the world and develop our country while giving jobs to poor as well.__Krishna DSRR

Giving government lands to poor people for less prices can avoid encroachers. Government also will get lot of money and good will which can be turn in to votes. Urbanizing possible twin cities can make many become rich. Rest can be cultivated land or forest.__Krishna DSRR

Possessiveness gives lot of pain creating doubts, questions come out of doubts lead to break up, So love your beloved ones but don't become possessive. We need space.__Krishna DSRR

Think logically, work hard to earn Name&money, spend those purposefully. These can make a person achieve anything, more importantly long lasting fame.__Krishna DSRR

Allowing others grow make us grow more bigger than them knowing their success story, by getting inspiration, by updating ourselves according to present situation to beat them to set new standard for new people to grow. Like this we can have lot of successful people.__Krishna DSRR

Notice everything to get knowledge about everything, edit bad forgetting, keep good to have a good future.__Krishna DSRR

Nothing is permanent in this universe even our planet 'Earth'. Because if any other planet hits it. It will become nothing. But we people always fight for life, properties, water, money, etc list goes on. So work hard to earn good name, be good to all to inspire them also. These give you immense happiness while doing and your name will last at least a 100 years even after death.__Krishna DSRR

Making C.E.O, senior managers of every company includes - all IT, Manufacturing, etc - open new company by giving loans will make us to see new: way of leader ship, Ideas, soft wares, products, and breaking old rules to form new ones to reach the expectations of new generations.__Krishna DSRR

Many soft wares can be created to accommodate our 120 crore people needs so we can start lot of new companies of our own to serve & earn people&money.__Krishna DSRR

Every body is dying with out fulfilling their dreams. That's why our population has been growing in Crores with rebirths. Hence, to control population we must make every body's dream come true. To do that we need to create an encouraging positive atmosphere.__Krishna DSRR

Money is the root cause of all evils but it is the root cause of all good too as many work hard to get much money, Pay taxes, later serve people.__Krishna DSRR

Love, Marriage, Children are great accidents-- these can change life positively or negatively to compromise or excel. Therefore, be careful "Drive Safe".___Krishna DSRR

Whether you succeed or fail but life will appreciate you when you experience every bit of it.__Krishna DSRR

Love gives pain, no love no pain. Life will be beautiful without love but if we take love from others that gives great happiness. So, don't love but be loved by others.__Krishna DSRR

TV can give life & death to your brain. It is the greatest invention on this earth.___Krishna DSRR

Every thing is unfinished in this world as it creates one more target in the name of updating to finish & gets criticism from opposition finding exemptions to be answered.

Hence, Be positive and keep going forward. You will have great life.____Krishna DSRR

We need to keep on achieve identity with good or bad till we get identity with our death. Then people come to say good bye remembering their good or bad time with us. We will be remembered as a good person for some, as a bad person for some. In this way we can be some thing achieving either good or bad identity, So we must do something without wasting time as If you be idle you get bad thoughts. Doing something will give practical experience, knowledge and lesson if its bad.__Krishna DSRR

The person you love will occupy you, make you loose friends, parents, relatives& more dangerously "Life" if that person rejects you. Be careful Love for Love only but not to give life. __Krishna DSRR

Adding more friends from all world let us have lot of experiences of different people from different world. It can be done through Social Media- Face Book, Instagram, traveling, studying abroad, etc.__Krishna DSRR

Once great people lived in this world they invented many. Now greatest people are living as these discovering many. I hope to see greater than people in future but I don't know what they will do, we have to wait and see.__Krishna DSRR

Love teaches us how to impress this world as well. So fall in love, raise in love and succeed in life.__Krishna DSRR.

I loved many but never expressed. so I am very happy as nobody rejected me.__Krishna DSRR

Age, Time can't be regained. Therefore, make use of experiencing every second, every feeling of age.__Krishna DSRR

Where ever you go you see good, bad. which one do you choose?. It depends upon the circumstances you face, but people appreciate, or blame you.__Krishna DSRR

Moon, sun who give day, night are always remain to watch what's going on earth. Ever green undying satellites. We must thank them for their surveillance.__Krishna DSRR

Done, done, done... we are Done with every second but we must start afresh in the next second.__Krishna DSRR.

God writes a different story for everyone, 'Oh my God' God is a great writer who can write world full of stories.__ Krishna DSRR

We get names like Honey, Bujji, Nani, Bunny, Chintu, Chinna, James, Srinu, Saleem & etc but a few people's name will be forever those who work for poor people like Mother Theresa, M.K.Gandhi (Father of India), Sardar Vallabhai Patel, Abraham Lincoln, Abdul Kalaam, Vajpayee, Narendra Modi.__Krishna DSRR

Hundreds of emotions daily, 'Oh my God' what a great species am I on this earth? We have been having an edge of the seat thriller kind of an emotional journey through out our life. Some say, Be careful thrillers can be dangerous but we can never be bored. And will have great results 'Brave, Brilliant' adjectives will be given by people. Hence choose this one or some other genre which suits you.__Krishna DSRR

Knowing who voted our party and members of our party is very important as we can serve them in all possible aspects. Then they will vote again remaining in our party or as common voter.__Krishna DSRR

Second, Minute, Hour, Day, Month, Year ......counting..counting....'Oh my God' Do we really need to hurry to die? Yes, we must hurry to work hard then our life can go jet speed till we die enormously.__Krishna DSRR

Swami Vivekananda said every one has God in him but its really difficult to find, show him to others. Because most of the people are negative thinkers. They name godly nature people as mad. But, if you are a positive thinker, you can see and be God.__Krishna DSRR

Getting results for our hard work in the form of Name, Money make us work more brilliantly to produce unmatched new outing which will benefit this world as well.__Krishna DSRR

Appearance gives good impression, expression gives better impression and reacting well gives the best impression.__Krishna DSRR

Parents give us birth to come into this beautiful world, we also give birth to our children to come but its really great to give birth to new ideas which will make all have great life in this wonder full world.__Krishna DSRR

Producing great humans inspiring common people comfort this world with new ideas, producing different new items comfort humans with new experience. But with every new comfort there will be a disadvantage but we have to move forward as we have Plus, Minus with every new invention.__Krishna DSRR

Crores of words from every language. So choosing right words according to the context will make us successful. Having balanced emotional journey allow us to have good perception to choose right words according to the context.__Krishna DSRR

Lighting up others lives surely burns our life. But it gives immense happiness which we can't even find in heaven.__Krishna DSRR

Exclude bad people, Excuse for fun, Excel positively then can have Excellent death Journey.__Krishna DSRR

Whatever you Express, Say and Do will have a reaction. Hence, be prepared to Express, Say and Do your reply.__ Krishna DSRR

If we know other's experiences, we will have good experiences. So, share yours and receive others giving/spending time.__Krishna DSRR

Its not about the money its about the life I want to live. For that I need money. For that I need to work hard. For that I need a healthy body, Soul. For that I need Yoga, Meditation. For that I don't need any thing and help from any one as I do yoga cum meditation when I don't have food, peace.__Krishna DSRR

New inventions can't be accepted immediately,

moreover, sometimes, the inventor can be prosecuted to death. But the invention will definitely be accepted some day when change required. Don't be discouraged as there is lot of necessity of inventors for this world.__Krishna DSRR.

Patience, Purity, and Perseverance are the secret of success in a good cause. Logical thinking, Hard work are the secret of success in general goals.__Krishna DSRR

Let the God come into your house continuing prayers at least once daily then no evil, evil thought can even think about coming near you and your house. Prayer is very powerful as where prayers are being offered, those people thoughts and that God related stories are the talk of the place. Like many say if we want success regarding something intently we automatically work hard and whole world will help us understanding our thoughts dnd that success will come to us. There is science behind this. Here it goes "Our thoughts will go like mobile signals through Air or through mind to mind and prepare this world to offer that success." So, prayer will make you have good, auspicious atmosphere around you and thinking for good achievements and always working hard for success will make this world give you that required success. Keeping, said, good atmosphere around you make you feel good and achieving great success let you and your country have respect, praise from this whole world.__Krishna DSRR

Don't follow like sheep do as your leader may cheat you. Its better question him Where to go? Why to go? How many possible ways to go to choose the best one? Proper and purposeful questions always help you and your leader as well. Help you from cheating by your leader. Help your leader in taking best suitable decision while leading you towards Goal. Encourages team work while fulfilling tasks. Democratic ways of discussions happen for our better future.__Krishna DSRR

Exclude bad people, Excuse for fun, Excel positively then can have Excellent death Journey.__Krishna DSRR

A thorough knowledge of Bible, Bhagavad Gita,

Khuran is worth more than a college education. And can become a saint. But must know how to preach and how to tell parables.__Krishna DSRR

Information is wealth. Information must be passed from one to another. A piece of information through any means can change your life. Like charitable trust address, Charitable Hospitals phone numbers, Orphanages, Temples which provide food for free whole week respectively Shiva on Monday, Anjaneya on Tuesday, Sai baba on Thursday, Lakshmi Devi on Friday, Venkateshwara on Saturday, etc.__Krishna DSRR

An art form ((architecture) a form of artistic expression (such as writing or painting or architecture), a video, a quote, an idea and a picture can make you get inspiration to refresh without getting bored of daily melancholy.__ Krishna DSRR

National feelings, Racial feelings, Regional feelings, Caste&Creed feelings, Gender feelings, Political Party feelings are the most important ones can make you Zero or Hero. Better consider only Good people and intelligent people for everything for a better society.__Krishna DSRR

True constructive criticism is always appreciated which will make us learn a lot to excel in future.__Krishna DSRR

If you are good enough to find good in every one, you will have whatever you want in life.__Krishna DSRR

Analyze the whole day before sleep. Good deeds, Bad deeds, which gave you happiness, sadness, reasons, solutions at least for half an our.__Krishna DSRR

Having many books around you won't give you knowledge. Reading one book at least twice will definitely make you acquire knowledge.__Krishna DSRR

Don't waste time because you won't get it back. Don't postpone anything because you won't get enough time to finish later.__Krishna DSRR

Life is not about finding yourself. Life is about creating yourself getting knowledge from everything. Knowing which interests you. Then everything falls in place.__Krishna DSRR

Don't lie to yourself compromising because if you start compromising while fulfilling your thoughts, dreams, it will go long till you die without fulfilling your thoughts, dreams.__Krishna DSRR

True Mysteries, Splendid landscapes, Mind blowing Views from mountains, Deep Valleys, Spacious Ponds, Lakes, River canals, Water falls, Beautiful shores, beautiful Sounds, Aromatic Smells, Fruits, Leaves, Medicine from different trees, Wildlife, Natural Wonders-Clouds, Clouds borne wonders, Lightnings, Thunders, Thunderbolts, Rainbows, Different types of Air, Air borne wonders, Different types of Rains, Rain borne wonders, through seasons even in metro cities only nature can make you experience all these through different seasons. May be sometimes disasters like cyclone, floods happen to cause lot of damage but It's only because of human negligence while building Roads and Buildings- No quality in materials and precautions to survive from natural disasters. Drainage system-- No quality, Not decaying wastage must be separated from decayable wastage then no hindrance to drainage water though they thrown it in drainage. Houses without water harvesting by building Wells/Pits to increase groundwater and prevent floods.__Krishna DSRR

Your friends don't need your explanation and your enemies won't believe you. Hence don't waste time in explanation.__Krishna DSRR

Feeding poor people through ration shops by governments, building houses for poor can make them have confidence and will be able to earn money through any job for buying T.V, Fridge, Double cot bed, Gold, etc list goes on. Government gets taxes. If we give free education for very poor people/fee reimbursement can help students become Graduates, Post Graduates. Literacy percentage grows. Students learn to use bank accounts. Banks can rotate that money for interest, etc. Those Graduates, Post Graduates can get jobs in any place through out the world. Some can be business men/women getting loans from banks, government, all possible sources. That country which possess Graduates, post graduates can get investments from across the globe. There will be lot of traveling for job searching, while doing job gets profits for Traveling agencies and Rental business will grow, and many more businesses and benefits.__Krishna DSRR

Unexpected customers who want to make us donate for their illness. We at least must inform the right place to be treated well. May be God have been sending them to make me be prepared if I get any illness then if I don't have enough money at least information that I got with me can help me. So keep list of Hospitals, Trusts, Orphanages, N.G.O organizations, etc philanthropists to help Poor people if required us.__Krishna DSRR

If we don't try, we won't get anything. Try, try, try until you get and do something. While trying you learn a lot and while doing you learn a lot both make you get perfection.__Krishna

DSRR

If we don't ask, the answer is always 'No'. If you ask there may be chances of 'Yes'. Ask your teacher when you get a doubt. Ask your friend when you have a problem. Ask your Girl Friend/Boy Friend to love or reciprocate. Ask your politicians to be answerable. This way your world and this whole world can be changed.__Krishna DSRR

Restricting Alcohol shops for Rich only will make poor people avoid drinking alcohol. But many don't want to quit alcohol as they have been earning money and enjoying spending that money. Only Poor people get benefit. Rest complain as they got control over their Financial, Family, Social life. These people hate Alcohol prohibition. Hence consider checking pan cards before selling alcohol to check customers financial status and to track drunkards who commit crimes.__Krishna DSRR

Issuing shares can make many become Millionaires, Billionaires. Hence every industry must issue shares then they also can reduce loss, if any recession they can face and more ideas having a team of share holders taking the company forward with team work begets good results.__Krishna DSRR

Until finishing Degree we must not allow any one to be in Film industry either it is Bollywood or Hollywood, or any Movie industry. Because they can't handle pressure of glamour industry filled with celebrities. Communication gap, Language problems. Immature nature of teenagers, Celebrities cosmopolitan nature can't match. Hence many of them getting problems. Celebrities getting problems by their(Immature) surviving tactics- creating problems between Director, Hero or Hero, Heroine and supporting one of them, Gossip mongering linking two opposite sex. When they know about those tactics, those illiterate cum immature people getting affected losing their life. Hence its better to finish at least Degree, learning required languages to be in Film industry. Then those can be mentally strong cum mature enough to handle any situation.__Krishna DSRR

If we don't think of new life and step forward,

we will be in the same boring life.__Krishna DSRR

Once a reader is now a famous writer, writing all genres of books. Once a listener is now a famous music director. Once a movie goer is now a Movie maker. Once, Now happens in every ones life which makes us remember past comparing with present and makes us become nostalgic. But when we are in a very good position now like I mentioned above everything looks brighter than past. Or else Uncontrollable pain.__Krishna DSRR

Constant perseverance in the same field made many reach top. You also can work hard sticking with one field then you will get the required perfection to bang this world with new ideas.__Krishna DSRR

Sharing Ideas make you have more Ideas, sharing emotions make you have more emotions, sharing experiences make you have more experiences, So the more you share the more you will get.__Krishna DSRR

Helping this universe will make you God, not

any other way or deed. It is the easiest method to be blissful from within, to be implored by people and ultimately be God to bless people with boons. If you observe or research the lives of God men/women in this universe, they did the same thing and have been doing the same from lakhs of years. Helping may have different ways : Some helped through spiritual teachings. Some helped through physical patience like serving common people like a nurse do. Some helped through donating/allotting Provisions, Money, Properties, Gold, Diamonds for people welfare. On the whole it can be Spiritual, Physical, Family, Financial.__Krishna DSRR

All religions say only one thing that is Be Good and Do Good. Being good, doing good with intelligence, witty nature can create a positive atmosphere to achieve anything and can even win our enemies.__Krishna DSRR

Tolerance towards other religions always makes our religion a great one. Religion mixed with science like healthy food offerings at Temple/Church/Masjid, Early morning prayers after head bath, Different types of bows, Walking around God, Chanting/psalm can make our brain cells be active as music do, Fasting, Meditation and Yoga all got scientific reasons to practice. Hence every religion with science can be implored.__Krishna DSRR

Donate blood for every three months which will make you save a life and your body produces new blood to make you more healthier than ever before.__Krishna DSRR

Every day has a festival or occasion or special day etc to celebrate. If you are a world citizen you have got to celebrate all days of whole year as festivals/Special days according to different Religions, Races, Castes, Creed, Political parties, etc hell of reasons. You may have to celebrate 2 or 3 festival in a single day. As we got many Religions, Races, Castes, Creed, Political parties, Ideologies, Countries, we got many festivals/special days.__Krishna DSRR

Parables are the main communicating tools to convey our messages, teachings. All our Gods used these creating fine ones. We also can create parables to inspire, to give examples, to entertain while writing if you are a writer/author, etc. Many speakers, writers, Authors, Self-help books authors, positive thinking books authors tend to use parables to inspire and exemplify experiences of others.__Krishna DSRR

Donating some percentage 30% or 70% of his company shares or of his whole wealth will get him good name as philanthropist and most people become followers to him and his all types of posts through Social media- Face Book, Twitter, Instagram,etc. Many want to join his company to work in a said professional working environment where they got a good sense of charity programs. This way Goodwill grows, share value grows and profits move forward by leaps and bounds. His quotes will be read, his experiences will be cherished, his suggestions will be followed and on the whole he can change many lives becoming a role model. So, I urge many rich become like this changing many lives.__Krishna DSRR

All Gods proposed democracy knowing the

body and soul of humans. Allah preached pray in the union of as many people as you can gather. Jesus also said Gather in a union and altogether pray keeping me in mind there I will live among with you. Work hard for you, your children then can pay taxes. Government can serve in return. Pray to god whenever you get time. Then I will be with you. Hindu gods like Krishna also said Pray in union there I will be with you. I am everything Preacher, Doer, Receiver, Warrior, King, Slave,etc all You just do what you would like to do. If you do good you will get good or you get bad. That means they have proposed democracy long ago. All said only one thing if 10 people decide something to do after discussing plus points and minus points. That must be done. It is what is democracy. Hence all Gods proposed democracy long ago but humans took time to have Democracy. All Gods, Prophets, Seers and Saints are Great Diplomats. Diplomatic approach can make you have required success.__Krishna DSRR

My 'Life' decided by me or my parents or this society. What I want? What my parents want?

What my society want? We must have a perfect balance with reasonable answers between these three very emotional aspects. Then can be something.__Krishna DSRR

Nothing happens when you don't work, Anything is possible if we work hard. Get as many skills as you wish to survive in this competitive world. Hard work beats all, like talented but stopped learning further, talented by robbing others, talented through shortcuts.__Krishna DSRR

Stressing all body muscles daily will make you lose fat and gives you healthy body, brilliant brain, Well-situated soul. All these can happen through practicing Yoga. Yoga is easy to practice, don't take much time, can be done any where without any assistance.__Krishna DSRR.

Many Clubs, Universities, Organizations, Societies are there to encourage winners but no body is there to create winners giving training, and all the requirements. I hope to see more winners will be created from all these 100s of Universities, Organizations,

Clubs, Societies.__Krishna DSRR

Every one in this world has something to do as their duty. So, knowing that you must finish your duty before your death. If you don't finish your duties you will have bad death journey or your children have got to finish. They will chide you. Hence finish your duties without postponing. Who knows what will happen next minute.__Krishna DSRR

Earning certificates give you respect but the gist which you learnt from courses can make you do your job well in real world. That is the reason why many people say certificates can be useful only to clean our tongue but talent got through practical knowledge, Practical thinking helps you survive in this Competitive, Target based World.__Krishna DSRR

Education gives you degree. It is just a piece of paper, Your education is seen in your behavior. To realize your inborn talent, to earn required good qualities for betterment of regularly changing society and to manifest the perfection already in you Education is required.__Krishna DSRR

Some students come to college to spend time with their friends, Some come to love some one, some come to watch/spend time with opposite sex, some come to play cricket/other game, Some come to spend time in library, Some come to learn from lectures of their faculty. Every one must go to college to get the required understanding of this society to face real world after studies, to get good percentage to be at par to get good job, to get good friends, if you fall in love you get a great lover cum would be life partner, Participation in cultural activities, NCC, Sports, etc all which can help you and this world as well.__Krishna DSRR

Possessiveness creates fear afterwards doubts. Giving space, Having space definitely allow us have a beautiful life.__Krishna DSRR

Change is required but in a positive way. Initially people may reject you but later they will love you and hail you.__Krishna DSRR

Many men think women want money, cars, and Gifts. But the right woman wants, A man's time effort, passion, honesty, smile, and him choosing to put her as his priority. Need to think about these only.__Krishna DSRR

Once T.V, now Mobiles, Tablets, I-pods, etc all electronic gadgets became a problem for having a good relationship with our Family, Relatives and Friends near by but useful when these are abroad or some where else having long distance. Hence use according to purpose.__Krishna DSRR

Love gives pain, no love no pain. Life will be beautiful without love but if we take love from others that gives great happiness. Therefore, don't love but be loved by others.__Krishna DSRR

When you want to achieve something, half of the Universe conspires in helping you to achieve it and at the same time half of the Universe conspires in discouraging you to loose hope of it. But it is you who can make this Universe fight having a great idea to achieve.__Krishna DSRR

Updating out of dated ones, discovering new ones based on existing ones, inventing new ones doing research always gets great results.__Krishna DSRR

Political Issues continue years as many politicians don't want to solve. Vote bank politics always a threat to democracy. When you get votes saying we solve particular problems, those must be solved before next election. Then can have new problem or else same problem same economy, same growth, same life of people. No moving forward in all aspects of development. Needless to say, when it comes to Politics every problem must be solved or else many, not only many a country and the whole world get bad results.__Krishna DSRR

Playing with life being Rich people, Super Rich. Taking satellite T.V watching everyone and everything sitting in the home these super Rich controlling this world. Hence be careful with life being Poor, Common man, Middle class, Upper Middle class.__Krishna DSRR

No action can give you freedom; Only knowledge can make you free. Can answer any problem/question in life, can get good job which will give us financial freedom, Can have good wife, later children and can transfer knowledge. As a result of knowledge we can have all types of freedom. Hence acquire as much knowledge as you can in any thing.__Krishna DSRR

The perfect never becomes imperfect. To be perfect you need constant practice and learning. Perfection can create wonders. Hence there is no going back.__Krishna DSRR

All condemnation of others really condemns ourselves. We must appreciate their plus points too. Then they try to have more plus points to make us feel bad and give us competition. In this we grow better and better criticizing, appreciating and getting the same from others.__Krishna DSRR

Choose the highest ideal and live your life up to that. You at least achieve something. Thats why many say 'Dream Big, Think Big and Work Hard'.__Krishna DSRR

Experience is the only teacher. But if you can learn from others suggestions, experiences, examples given by them. You will save lot of time and can achieve a lot in life before death.__Krishna DSRR

The greatest sin is to think yourself weak. Everyone in this Universe has their own plus points and minus points. Knowing those, increase plus points and reduce minus points. In this process you become very strong to achieve any thing. Without comparing with others you keep on achieving one by one competing with you only. One day you will be like the great Everest. No body can reach, but only a few.__Krishna DSRR

Don't spend your energy in talking, but meditate in silence. Don't waste your time Wondering, Gossiping. Its better to sleep to recharge your brain or at least read news paper or most importantly meditate.__Krishna DSRR

Hold your money merely as custodian for what is God's. As it goes to many places and to many pockets of people we must not feel that its our permanent possession. It belongs to God. Hence it goes to one person to another. Money must travel in exchange of something or else development stops. Therefore money must be spent purposefully.__Krishna DSRR

How can we see evil unless it is in us? See only God in every man, Woman and child. Don't let evil come into a person creating that situation. Misleading, irritating, humiliating without a reason, Snubbing unnecessarily, etc bad qualities make others become evil against you and this world.__Krishna DSRR

Meditation is on a series of objects; concentration on one object. So, Meditate to know about all and concentrate on one to achieve it.__Krishna DSRR

Truth must have no compromise. Follow truth it will take you till you achieve glorious victories in life. Believe in truth, it lead you to pinnacle of success.__Krishna DSRR

No two people see the same world. As their perceptions differ they see different worlds. The God who writes our story before birth writes a different story for everyone. Its really a great world with full of stories and full of different perceptions to know, understand and pursue. You can start from your home right away.__Krishna DSRR

Cleanse the mind, this is all of religion. Its true when you get a bad thought you can remember a god or Prayer to him, a chanting/psalm can change your mind towards good thoughts and deeds. Hence to cleanse the mind and rejuvenate our soul we need to follow a religion.__Krishna DSRR

No man/woman should be judged by his defects. We must judge anyone by his good qualities then he will try to be more good. We need to suggest solutions for others defects but not criticize. Praising good qualities, suggesting solutions for others defects can always make you get many friends.__Krishna DSRR

The human form is the highest and man the greatest being. Who can correct the present system and can create a new system. This Universe belongs to and ruled by Humans. Whatever happens in this Universe its mostly because Of Humans. Hence, Save this Universe without   polluting   it.   Its   your responsibility.__Krishna DSRR

Never lose faith in yourself; you can do anything in the Universe. Start learning from scratch later you will reach then pinnacle of knowledge. Knowledge gives confidence to achieve anything. So, have faith start over at any situation.__Krishna DSRR

Inspiration is much higher than reason, but it must not contradict it. Must have one more to continue our journey towards success. Later one more to continue that success.__Krishna DSRR

Man must love others, because those others are himself. When you love others you will start loving yourself. As others say positive points about you when you are in love with them. You also say good about them. In this way they know a lot about them Good and Bad. And you about yourself Good and Bad. Falling love make you love yourself, this world, your family, your lover the most. Love leads to love.__Krishna DSRR

Religious teaching must always be constructive, not destructive. Must lead towards good thinking, must show the path to live with hope, must show the way to have a job. Having staff to take care of visitors problems knowing their address, providing job information, giving loans from earnings through donations, creating groups at village level and cooperation between those groups in providing jobs, starting new businesses sharing investment. Like this many must be done. All religions first must provide livelihood then later spiritual journey.__Krishna DSRR

Imagination will lead you to the highest even more rapidly and easily than reason. Then at least live in imagination avoiding bad devil thoughts like an idle man/woman. Imagination is the birth place of many stories which got great success as movies throughout the world. And birth place of many discoveries, inventions. Imagination for the good of this world always be welcomed.__Krishna DSRR

The life is short, the vanities of the world are transient, but they alone live who live for others, the rest are more dead than alive. Many rich don't think about anyone else except themselves as they earned that rich status through hard work. They say everyone must work hard. But everyone must need a helping hand in creating opportunities or giving jobs. Therefore at least become a helping hand   passing   information,   showing opportunities, giving jobs in the own company, giving loans to create new businesses. Providing schools, colleges, adopting villages etc many ways are there to make your life worth living. You can live even after death.__Krishna DSRR

Character alone can make you have good friends, supporters. They will be ready at any time to help you as a pay back. Have good character, earn people then you will have good life.__Krishna DSRR

My method of work is to construct and not pull down. I always love to construct a relationship, construct a building, construct a good system to have happy fulfilling life. But those who always look for destruction can't have people around him. Please stay away from those type of people.__Krishna DSRR

We only get what we deserve. Don't look for more than your hard work. Your character, hard work decide the eligibility in achieving the range of success. The more good you are, the more you work hard, the more successful you will be.__Krishna DSRR

Throughout the history of mankind, if any motive power has been more potent than another in the lives of all great men and women, it is that of faith in themselves. As many say have faith in yourself you can achieve any thing and can become one of the great. Many situations come to make you lose confidence in you. But every situation has an ending which will make you realize your strength to achieve any thing.__Krishna DSRR

There is nothing holier in the world than to keep good company. If you are good and got good company you don't need to visit temple or any holy place. God himself come to you and live with you.__Krishna DSRR

Neither seek nor avoid: take what comes. This is freedom----to be affected by nothing. Converting what comes to you into your opportunity to excel in life can always make you have positive results to succeed in life.__Krishna DSRR

Stay focused in your profession and expand your ideas to reach the whole world then everyone come to you to have your association.__Krishna DSRR

A man who spends his time in discussing the good and bad qualities of others simply wastes his own time. If he thinks about himself instead he can do wonders and later he can easily understand others to win their heart as well.__Krishna DSRR

Don't let worldly thoughts and anxieties disturb your mind. Be focused on your goal. It can be Spiritual or Financial or Family or Social. When you reach your goal rest of the desires, goals, thoughts can be fulfilled.__Krishna DSRR

It is glorious to help even one man in my whole life. The capability of helping others is a boon which we must not miss the opportunity to help the needy.__Krishna DSRR

He alone is the true teacher who is illumined by the light of true Knowledge. And who can impart that knowledge impartially is a true guru. Who will be revered by many throughout and even after his life. What a simple living and great achievement of a teacher indeed.__Krishna DSRR

Holy men are born on earth to show people the way to God. People wish strongly, When this world required a holy man/woman to purify and enlighten the minds and hearts of people. They teach differently according to living time. There are many paths leading to the same goal. Therefore the teachings of all the saints are true.__Krishna DSRR

How can the devotees really have any caste? Children are all equal for God to bless them. Caste, Creed or else nothing can stop you in reaching God and God's living place (a Temple, Church, Shrine, Masjid).__Krishna DSRR

Many are known to do great works under the

stress of some strong emotion. 'An emotional journey' which can make us achieve any thing in this world. We must be connected emotionally to our achievements then can easily be achieved.__Krishna DSRR

One must experience the effect of past action. None can escape it. But prayer minimizes its intensity. Many said Prayer has lot of power. So, everyone must pray to some God or the other.__Krishna DSRR

The Christian is not to become a Hindu or a Buddhist, not a Hindu or a Buddhist to become a Christian. But each must assimilate the spirit of the others and yet preserve his individuality and grow according to his own law of growth.__Krishna DSRR

Take up one idea. Make that one idea your life----think of it, dream of it, live on that idea. Let the brain, muscles, nerves, every part of your body, be full of that idea, and just leave every other opposite idea and add every supporting idea. This is the way to success.__Krishna DSRR

Good motives, sincerity, and infinite love can conquer the world. One single soul possessed of these virtues can destroy the dark designs of millions of hypocrites and brutes.__Krishna DSRR

The uplift of the women, the awakening of the masses must come first, and then only can any real good come about for the country, for India and the whole world.__Krishna DSRR

India will be raised, not with the power of flesh, but with the power of the spirit; not with the flag of destruction, but with the flag of peace and love.... Say not that you are weak. The spirit is omnipotent. Don't need to worry about Christian churches built and preachings there. All religions have their Offices called Temples, Ashrams, Churches, Monasteries, and all those represent different religions.__Krishna DSRR

The first priority of life is expansion. You must expand if you want to live. The moment you have ceased to expand, death is upon you, danger is ahead. To be more clear you must be broadminded to receive any new positive thought, apply those and to give any new positive thought, see those be applied. More importantly expand your friend circle throughout the world. Now its pretty easy. They can be relatives, can be soul mates , can be in any good relationship with you in the process.__Krishna DSRR

The eyes of the whole world are now turned towards this land of India for spiritual food; and India has to provide it for all the races. Here alone is the best ideal for mankind; and Western Scholars are now striving to understand this ideal which is enshrined in our Sanskrit literature and philosophy, and which has been the characteristic of India all through the ages. It is said by Swami Vivekananda and its happening even now. Many countries have been inviting our Spiritual Leaders to have training to be Spiritual pursuers.__Krishna DSRR

Bring light to the poor, and bring more light to the rich, for they require it more than the poor; bring light to the ignorant and more light to the educated as the Rich and Educated got lot of pride which can be Ego. Ego ruins many lives very easily without any reason. Thus bring light to all and leave the rest unto the Lord.__Krishna DSRR

It is a tremendous error to feel helpless. Do not seek help from anyone. We are our own help. If we can't help ourselves, there is none to help us. Start helping yourself now through Yoga, Meditation which can be done with less energy, anywhere, at any time and which can change your life forever.__Krishna DSRR

Education is not the amount of information that is put into your brain and runs riot there, undigested, all your life. We must have life-building, man-making, character-making, assimilation of ideas.__Krishna DSRR

In India there are two great evils. Trampling on the women, and suppressing the poor through caste restrictions. These two bad qualities of Indians made foreigners rule India for many years. Hence, respect Women and help Poor without any partiality through giving Rights, Charity or Welfare schemes to be well educated, well fed, and well cared for.__Krishna DSRR

Each generation should be inspired afresh. Or else can have problems because this world has been getting changes daily.__Krishna DSRR

Everyone got good and bad in him. If you show good to people, then people call you Good man and God. If you show bad, then people call you bad man and Devil. Its all in your hands. Misunderstandings may happen but at the end Good will win.__Krishna DSRR

Give up the awful disease that is creeping into our national blood, that idea of ridiculing everything, that loss of seriousness. Give that up. Be strong and have 'Attention', and everything else is bound to follow.__Krishna DSRR

Political greatness or military power is never the mission of our nation, it never was, and mark my words, it must be. Because to protect us from others, not like before allowing others to rule us. But there has been the other mission given to us, which is to conserve, to preserve, to accumulate and to spread all the spiritual energy of our Nation. The land where humanity has attained its highest towards gentleness, towards generosity, towards purity, towards calmness, above all, the land of introspection and of Spirituality, It is India.__Krishna DSRR

Men/Women should be taught to be practical and physically strong. A dozen of such lions can conquer this Universe, and not millions of sheep can do so. Secondly, Men/Women should not be taught to imitate a personal ideal, however great.__Krishna DSRR

Romance rejuvenates passion, making one's sex life more interesting. Sexual ignorance is a social disease and can only be resolved through comprehensive interesting and interested partner. When you have good sex life getting educated from Vastyana Kama Sutra or something else like this from some country, you can have healthy and energetic life. Which can make you have successful career.__Krishna DSRR

Anyone who stops learning is old whether at twenty or eighty. Any one who keeps learning stays young.__Krishna DSRR

All our dreams can come true if we work hard to achieve them.__Krishna DSRR

In the middle of difficulty lies opportunity. Hence, be optimistic then you can understand and grab that opportunity.__Krishna DSRR

The quickest way to correct the other fellows attitude is to correct your own first. Then he will change seeing your change automatically.__Krishna DSRR

It is a fact that you project what you are. Thus the greatest mistake a person can make is doing nothing. If you earn something through hard work you can project well.__Krishna DSRR

My best friend is the one who brings out the best in me. Who can make me realize what I am and make me be down to earth. He is the one who always supports me while explaining positive and negative results. And always proposes to do good avoiding bad.__Krishna DSRR

The business of life is to go forward. Never ever lose any small opportunity to continue that progress. If regression starts people laugh at you to kill you mentally which may lead to death of you and your entire businesses.__Krishna DSRR

Lost time cannot be recovered. Thus, without wasting time, try to utilize every minute to learn something in achieving your goals. After reaching your goals, you can enjoy a perfectly planned fun filled vacation.__Krishna DSRR

Our greatest glory is not in never failing but in rising up every time we fail. Failing, failing must lead you to learning. Learning, learning lead you to perfection. When you get perfection nobody or nothing can stop you have a successful life.__Krishna DSRR

Your problem is not your problem. Your attitude how you handle your problems Is your problem. Don't find fault, find remedy. Positive attitude always work.__Krishna DSRR

Ninety nine percent of failures come from people who have the habit of making excuses.

You better excuse those people solving problems created by them. Find new people who work hard.__Krishna DSRR

A danger foreseen is half avoided. Logical thinking, analytical skills can make us estimate/ see the future. Hence we can plan accordingly.__Krishna DSRR

They are rich who have true friends. To feel is good, to think is better, to speak is far better but to do is the best of all. The most precious gift of nature is a friend with a cheerful, jesting and kind mind.__Krishna DSRR

Women's anger is like a diamond's glitter, it only shines but cannot burn.__Krishna DSRR

To be happy, you must learn to forget your past or forgive yourself. Remembering God or good feelings wash away unpleasant reactions.__Krishna DSRR

Happiness depends on what you can give, not what you can get. You get a lot from this world but when you give back you feel so happy making this world also feel so happy taking from you.__Krishna DSRR

Count your days by friends, not years. Have as many friends as you can to have as many lessons from experiences of your friends as you can knowing and from some of your experiences with them. Now-a-days Social media helps a lot to have many friends along with schools, Colleges, Communities.__Krishna DSRR

Reading makes a full man, conference a ready man, writing an exact man. Read as many books as you can and understand Past, Present, Future using imagination. Conference makes you express, writing makes you confirm your understanding. Plan based on that understanding, You can surely have a great prosperous life.__Krishna DSRR

Facts are stubborn things. But rules can be broken. But must be broken replacing a new idealistic rule which can make us have good going in life.__Krishna DSRR

Travel teaches toleration. It makes you know yourself giving you enough loneliness. Makes you know different cultures, societies, and complete different worlds. Makes you know how different worlds function which makes you have wonderful world of your own.__Krishna DSRR

When we die money don't come with us. Relatives, friends only come until graveyard. But Good deeds and bad deeds we did in the whole life will make us live even after death in the memories of people. They talk about us and our Ideas. They celebrate our birth and death anniversary.__Krishna DSRR

Common sense is the most uncommon commodity in the world. Have common sense and if you can control all your senses you can create wonders. Which will make you happy satisfying all your senses.__Krishna DSRR

Leaders assume mastery by looking at reality through different lenses. Thinking about a topic in 10 ways can make you have new ideas. Leaders listen, observe and think to succeed.__Krishna DSRR

All animals except Humans know that the

ultimate point of life is to enjoy it. Humans look for immense happiness from within which comes when you fall in love for the first time, When you achieve your goal, When you get great respectable fame which can long even after your death. When people hail you with superlative phrases.__Krishna DSRR

Don't wait for leaders, do it alone person to person. Then you can be leader. And can make many become leaders letting them take initiative. If you start helping yourself your leaders will come to help you further. Even God also can't help who doesn't help themselves.__Krishna DSRR

Anger is one word (letter or alphabet) short of Danger. So, have a talk instead to excel further in life.__Krishna DSRR

Its better to be criticized than to be ignored. Mistakes give punishment along with lessons. Those lessons can change your lives positively.__Krishna DSRR

Don't go by the looks, go by the qualities. Looks fade away, but qualities may remain. If updated or replaced those qualities must be with more good ones only. Hence qualities touch heart and win hearts.__Krishna DSRR

Leadership comes not always from taking leadership. But more often from giving leadership away. Leadership sharing/ Power sharing always yields good results. Many take the leadership, feel responsible and work hard to win the hearts of the voters.__Krishna DSRR

The best way to know God is to love many things. Love many people seeing by searching God in them. If you look for God in all, one day you will definitely find the God from many.__Krishna DSRR

The cure for boredom is curiosity. There is no cure for curiosity. Always in search of learning or knowing new things make you be busy and gives you lot of joy which will be appreciated by many.__Krishna DSRR

Be yourself. The world worships the original. Don't copy but know what has been going on through research. After knowing well the existing trend create a new trend in any field you like.__Krishna DSRR

Knowing is not enough, we must apply. Willing is not enough, we must do.__Krishna DSRR

The hand that rocks the cradle can rule the world. As Mother is the first teacher of any child. And teachers at school also plays an important role without showing any pampering, trains us to face the world. As Example is better than precept, at school many examples shown by our teachers using our friends.__Krishna DSRR

Checking our Voter ID, PAN card, Aadhaar card, Driving license, Bank account, Properties details to curb black money and to make people pay all taxes properly. Encouraging people to use all these cards as per the situations. Money must flow from one to another. Then only a country and world get the required development in all industries. Its very essential to make these happen.__Krishna DSRR

A person who can serve this world but not serving is more dangerous than a Terrorist.

Example: Many rich can serve this world starting a trust. Giving food, education to (Poor) backward children and spiritual knowledge can make those children build a great nation. In return he can get Goodwill which can be termed as an asset. Terrorist only can kill a few but this rich man can build a great nation which later can create a great world. Therefore if he doesn't do that he can be considered more dangerous than a terrorist.__Krishna DSRR

We are manufactured through our parents to be customers in this Universe. Being a new customer I bought Food, Education from school, college. Later a manufacturer of products or service if its service industry job. Afterwards marrying female customer turned producer/manufacturer we deliver a new customer or two. At this time we are being paid for doing jobs and that is being spent for delivered children. After earning money we give charity and later we can be joined in those old age homes making us new customers there because our children have new customers in the form of their children. The more customers we   produce   the   more   businesses flourish.__Krishna DSRR

Thanks & Regards,

Krishna DSRR